The Rodent, the Bee, and the Brazil Nut Tree

How Living Things Work Together for Survival

Sheri Amsel

For my little explorers:
Indiana, Leia, Fenix, Drake, and Eleni

I would also like to acknowledge my friend and science educator extraordinaire, Alexandria Siy. Our brainstorming hikes helped launch this story and many others.

Deep in the Amazon, the mighty Brazil nut tree towers over the rest of the jungle. This is the only place on Earth where Brazil nuts grow.

Their seed pods are as big as a grapefruit, as hard as stone, and can weigh up to five pounds each. When a seed pod drops from a Brazil nut tree, it crashes to the ground like a cannonball.

Every year, people come into the rainforest to collect the fallen seed pods and harvest the delicious Brazil nuts inside. They've learned to wait until all the seed pods have dropped before going into the forest to find them because of the *real* danger of being hit by a falling seed pod.

In one year, a single Brazil nut tree can grow about 250 pounds of these valuable nuts. Farmers have tried to grow Brazil nuts on tree farms, but it doesn't work. Brazil nut trees won't grow nuts without the help of a small rainforest creature, the orchid bee.

Brazil nut trees flower every year at the beginning of the rainy season. They have to be pollinated to grow seeds and there isn't much time. Each bloom lasts for just one day!

The flowers are big and tightly coiled with a heavy hood covering the opening. There are few insects big and strong enough to enter the blossoms...

...but the female orchid bee is capable.

Orchid bees are large and quite beautiful with shimmering, metallic green bodies.

They also have a very long, thin tongue that can reach down into the coiled flower to find the nectar. As it collects nectar, the flower's pollen brushes against the bee's back and clings there.

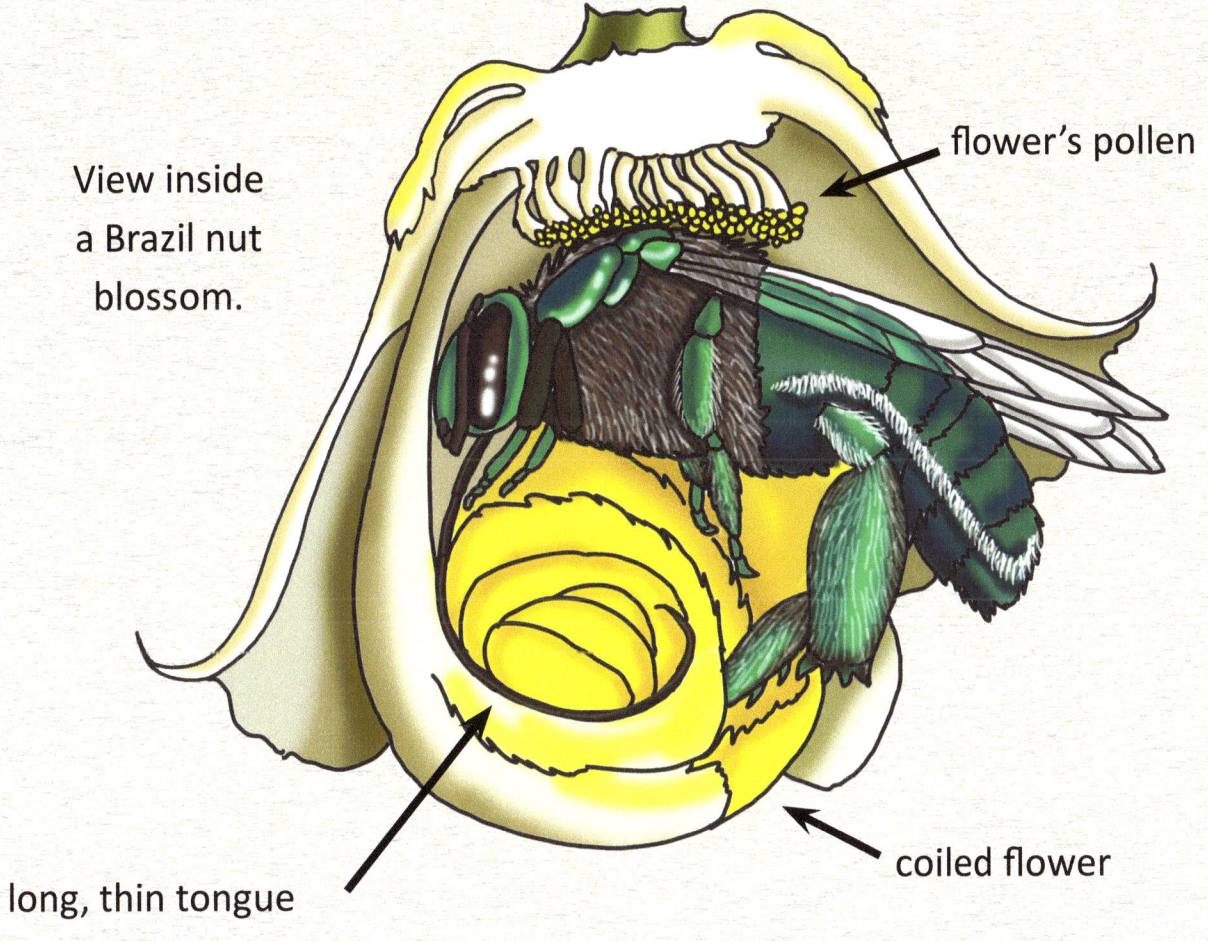

View inside a Brazil nut blossom.

flower's pollen

coiled flower

long, thin tongue

The bees then fly to the next blossom, and the next and the next, pollinating as they go.

Orchid bees don't live everywhere. They are only found in wild rainforests that are home to a special kind of beautiful, smelly orchid.

This orchid is from the group *Coryanthes*, which means *helmet flower*.

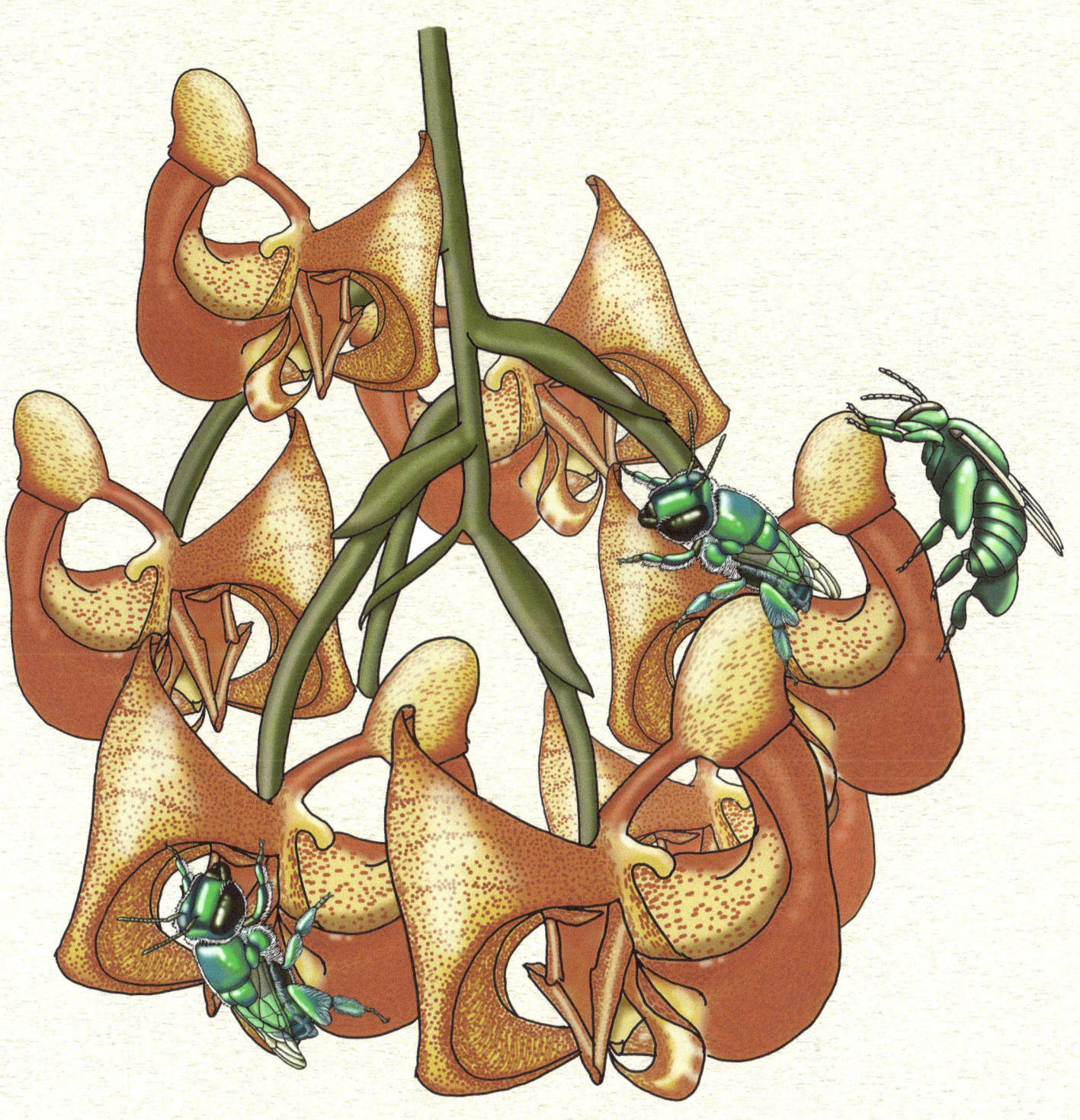

The male orchid bees pollinate these strange flowers and get covered by their strong scent and color. This smell attracts the female orchid bees to mate.

The orchid flower, in turn, needs lots of wild rainforest in which to grow.

It's interesting to think that to survive, a plant (the Brazil nut tree) depends on an insect (the bee) which depends on another plant (the orchid).

It is not unusual for different living things to help each other survive. Scientists call this process *mutualism*.

The seed pods of the Brazil nut tree also need help to release their seeds. A large rodent, called an *agouti*, gnaws open the thick seed pods with their sharp, chisel-like teeth to reach the two dozen delicious seeds inside.

The agouti will eat some seeds and bury the rest. Then, one day, when there is enough sunlight and moisture, the buried seeds may grow into new Brazil nut trees. That is why the agouti are also called *seed spreaders*.

The reason Brazil nut tree farms fail is because they need a natural ecosystem – flowers need the bees, bees need the orchids, and orchids need the rainforest.

As more and more of the rainforest is burned or cut down, this delicate ecosystem is at risk. The agouti, orchids, and bees will be lost, and it is likely that Brazil nuts may also disappear...forever.

Identifying and Finding Species

Use the following visual guide to identify 26 plants and animals found throughout the book.
Note that each plant and animal may be found on multiple pages. Can you find them all?

Agouti · Brazil Nut Flower · Brazil Nut Pod · Bromeliad

Butterfly (Glasswing) · Butterfly (Julia) · Butterfly (Kite Swallowtail) · Butterfly (Morpho)

Butterfly (Owl) · Butterfly (Sulfur) · Capybara · Cattleya Orchid

For Educators and Parents

In the following pages, learn more about how living things interact and their relationships with one another.

1) **Learn** about different kinds of symbiotic relationships among living things in the Amazon Rainforest.

2) **Research and Develop** a Pollination Poster (Mutualistic Activity).

3) **Investigate** Seed Dispersal (Commensalism Activity).

4) **Play** a Game of Tick Tag (Parasitic Activity).

5) **Creat**e an Amazon Rainforest Animal Journal.

6) **Solve** the Rainforest Hidden Picture.

7) **Draw** an Agouti using the step-by-step guide.

8) **Learn** about some of the birds, mammals, and insects found in the Amazon Rainforest.

How Living Things Interact

Living things interact with each other in different ways. One example is the predator-prey relationship. The jaguar preys on a capybara to feed itself and its young. It doesn't help an individual capybara to be eaten by a jaguar, but it may impact the overall capybara population by eliminating weak, sick, or injured members.

Other living things are often in competition with each other for resources. Fruit-eating monkeys all search for ripe fruit in the rainforest canopy and compete to eat it first.

Some very different creatures form close relationships to the benefit of one of the species. While it always benefits one, the relationship may help, hurt, or have no effect on the other. These symbiotic relationships are (or can be) broken down into mutualism, commensalism, and parasitism.

In **mutualism**, both living things benefit from their relationship. In the story of the Brazil nut tree, several species have developed mutualistic relationships. The Brazil nut tree benefits from the female orchid bees' pollination, while the bees benefit from the nectar they collect. Likewise, the agoutis benefit from the Brazil nuts they eat while the tree population benefits from the seeds that are planted.

Male orchid bees pollinate orchids and attract a mate.

Female orchid bees pollinate Brazil nut tree blossoms.

Agoutis open Brazil nut seed pods, eating some and burying others.

In **commensalism**, one species will benefit while the other is not affected by the interaction. An example of commensalism in the rainforest are bromeliads. These plants that grow up in the canopy take root on tree branches. They collect enough rainwater and sunlight to survive, but do not hurt or help the trees on which they grow. Another example are the small rainforest frogs that live inside bromeliads. They find water that pools down in the center of the leaves. They shelter there and find insects that have fallen into the water to eat. The frogs do not hurt the plant at all.

In **parasitism**, one species, called the parasite, lives off another species, called the host. The parasite benefits to the detriment of the host. Parasites can attach to a host internally or externally. A strange example of parasitism in the rainforest is a fungus that infects the brains of carpenter ants. The fungus programs the ant to anchor itself to a leaf by biting its main leaf vein with its mandibles. As the fungus grows, it bursts out of the ant's head, killing the unfortunate ant. The fungus then releases its spores. The spores rain down into the forest to infect any unsuspecting ants that happen to be down below, beginning the cycle all over again.

Research and Develop a Pollination Poster (Mutualistic Activity)

As we covered earlier, mutualism is a symbiotic relationship where species interact and benefit each other. A common example of this is when bees and other animals pollinate flowers. The flowers are fertilized and develop fruit and seeds, and the animals that pollinate the flowers receive nectar and pollen to eat.

Objective: Learn about pollination with a team and create an illustrated poster showing your discoveries.

Materials:

- access to online facts about pollination
- poster board
- drawing materials (markers, colored pencils, etc.)
- white paper
- glue stick
- scissors

Procedures:

1. Choose a team of classmates, friends, or siblings with whom you can work.
2. Decide who is best suited to research the topic (researcher), write down the important facts about pollination (recorder), and draw a diagram of each of the pollination facts (illustrator).
3. Work together to review the pollination facts collected by the researcher. Using your own words, define the facts that will go on the poster. Additionally, discuss how many images will need to be drawn to tell your pollination story.
4. Record/write each fact in marker on the white paper in little blocks of text that can be cut out and pasted onto the poster board beside the corresponding drawings.
5. Find a creative way to illustrate each fact on the poster board, leaving room for the text to be added. Outline the drawings in black marker and color them in.
6. Paste on the facts.

Discussion: Congratulations! You have created an informational poster about mutualism while simultaneously working together in a mutualistic interaction. Did you notice that while you were learning about mutualism you were also *engaging* in it with your teammates?

Seed Dispersal Investigation (Commensalism Activity)

Commensalism is a symbiotic relationship where one species will benefit while the other is not affected by the interaction. An example of this is seen in some forms of seed dispersal. In this investigation, you will see the interesting adaptations that plants have developed to spread their seeds by attaching to passing animals. This activity is most effective in late summer, depending on your location.

Objective: Learn about seed dispersal by performing an experiment mimicking a seed-spreading technique found in nature. Witness commensalism in action.

Materials:
- scissors
- old white sock
- plant mister
- flower pot full of damp potting soil, uncut grassy field, and/or wetland in late summer

Procedures:
1. Put a sock on one hand and walk through the tall vegetation, sweeping the sock-covered hand through tall grass, bushes, sedges, etc. Bend down and sweep through plants closer to the ground as well.
2. Once the sock has collected an assortment of seeds, cut it up and place the pieces in a pot full of damp soil.
3. Mist the sock until it is damp every day (not soaking wet). Place the pot in a sunny spot.
4. Over the next couple of weeks, mist the sock every day. Note if there is any green growth.
5. After a few weeks, observe the plant growth on the sock. Think about how the seeds would have been spread by animals in nature in the same way.

Discussion: Think about the physical characteristics seeds require to spread from one place to another.

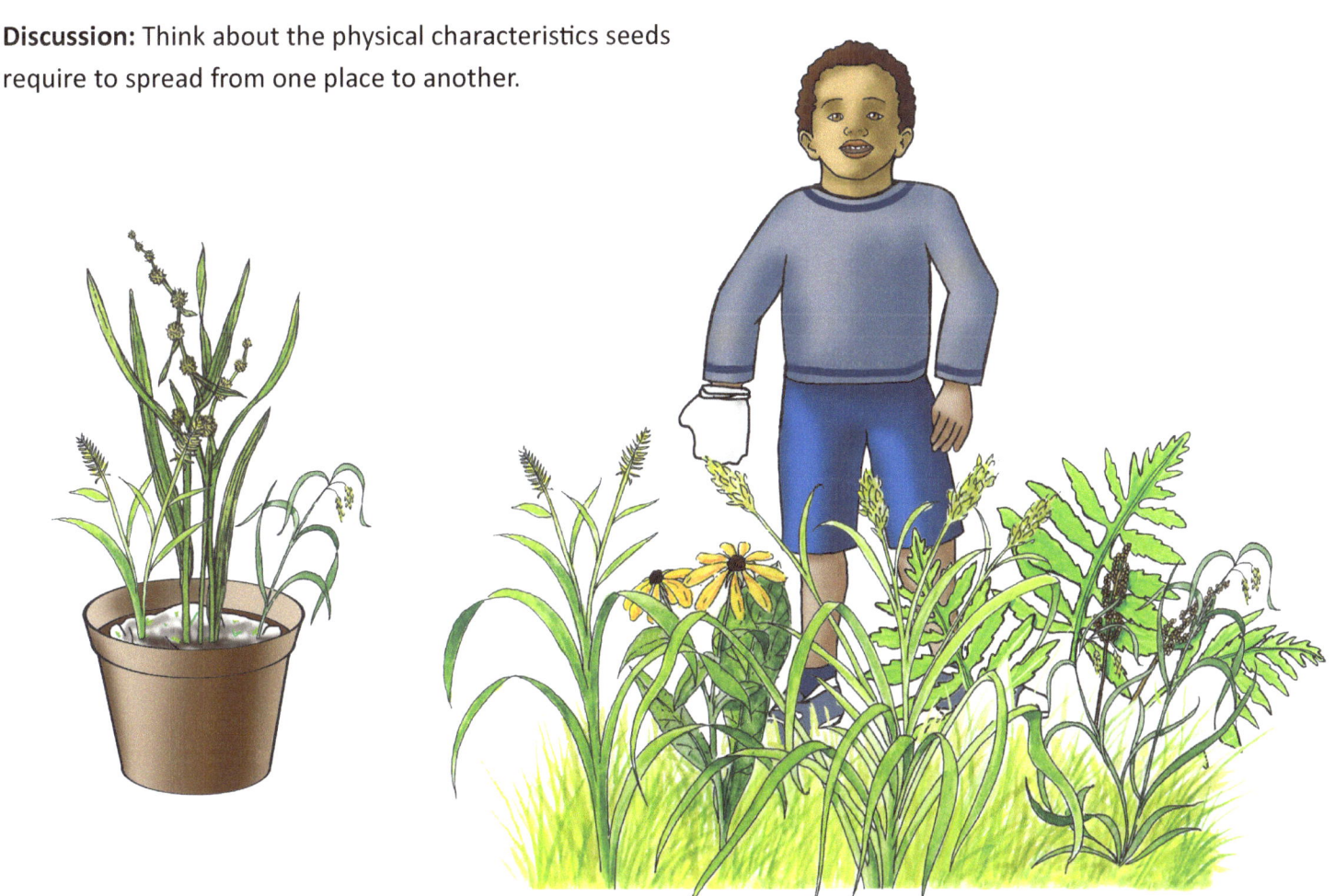

Tick Tag (Parasitic Activity)

Ticks attach to warm-blooded animals and feed on their blood to the detriment of the host. They sometimes transmit diseases, such as Lyme's.

Objective: Players learn about how wildlife accumulate ticks in the wild that can threaten their health and sometimes their lives.

Materials:

- sticky tags   • an open area to run around

Directions: This activity is for several people to play together, plus a supervisor to make sure no one is slapping tags on too forcefully. Supply more sticky tags, as needed. Announce when the "wildlife" has been compromised by parasites and the round is over.

1. Choose who will be the first wild animal (e.g., any warm-blooded animal like a deer, moose, raccoon, coyote, fox, rabbit, etc.).
2. Set the boundaries on the playing field so the "wild animal" knows where he/she/they can run.
3. The ticks chase the "wild animal," tag it with a sticky, and run back to the supervisor to get another and try again.
4. Each turn ends when the "wildlife" has more than 20 tags (you can change this number as needed).
5. Take turns with all players being a wild animal once. (The wild animal should not pull off the tags, just run.)

Discussion: In real life, wildlife brushes against grass or shrubs where ticks lie in wait. Grabbing the animal's fur, ticks latch onto the skin and feed on their blood. This game is meant to enable a discussion about ticks (parasitism) and safety measures people can take to protect themselves from tick-borne diseases.

Make a Rainforest Animal Journal

To learn more about rainforest animals, do some research and create your own rainforest journal.

Materials:
- white construction paper (2 or more sheets folded)
- rainforest animal pictures online, printed and cut out
- white paper
- stapler
- scissors
- white pencil
- glue
- black marker

Directions:

1. Fold construction paper in half vertically to make a 5.5" x 8.5" booklet with eight pages (add more paper if desired).
2. Find Amazon Rainforest animal pictures that you want to learn about online. Print and cut them out.
3. Paste each on one page in your journal. Be sure to leave room on the top or bottom of the page for the text you will write about each animal.
4. Draw a background in colored pencil or marker.
5. Research each animal and write some of their interesting characteristics on a square of white paper that will fit on the journal page. Paste it on the page.
6. Add a folded cover if you wish.
7. To keep your pages together, you can staple the journal booklet along the folded edge (optional).

Discussion: Share what you've discovered about these rainforest animals with your class. Did you learn anything that surprised you?

Rainforest Hidden Picture

Find eight things that people might carry while hiking in the rainforest: a backpack, a hat, bug repellant, a pocketknife, a shovel, rope, silverware, and a brush.

Learn to Draw an Agouti

Grab a pencil and a blank sheet of paper and follow these step-by-step instructions to draw an agouti.

Amazon Rainforest Mammals

Agouti live in the Amazon rainforests of Brazil, hiding in thick brush near rivers, streams, and swamps. They are small, shy rodents that eat only plants, fruits, and seeds. They bury leftover seeds for later, which often grow into trees, so they have earned the nickname *seed spreader*.

Capybara live in thick, brushy areas (always near water) of the Amazon rainforest in Central and South America. They are the largest rodents in the world, weighing up to 140 pounds. They are active mostly at night eating plants that grow in the water, grass, fruit, and tree bark.

Jaguars live in rainforests, scrublands, and swamps from Mexico to Northern South America. They can be up to eight feet long (including their tail) with markings that are actually rings with spots inside them. They hunt capybara, wild pigs, crocodiles, and rodents.

Spider Monkeys live in the rainforest from Mexico to Brazil. They have long, thin arms and legs and a very long tail that can grasp like a hand (prehensile) and carry the weight of their whole body. Spider monkeys live high in trees, sometimes 100 feet above the ground, eating fruit, nuts, seeds, leaves, insects, and even small animals.

Squirrel Monkeys live in rainforests from Costa Rica to central South America. They live high up in rainforest trees, only rarely coming down to the forest floor for food. They eat mostly insects but also ripe fruit.

Tapirs live in dense rainforests, in river basins, or near the swamps and rivers of southern Mexico down to Brazil. They are huge, weighing up to 900 pounds, and are excellent swimmers. Tapirs can dive into water and stay under for several minutes to escape predators. If they feel threatened when they are away from water, their large size allows them to barrel through dense brush to escape.

Amazon Rainforest Birds

Harpy Eagles live in forests from Central America down to South America. They are very large eagles, growing to 3.5 feet tall and have a large head crest. These eagles have short wings, so they can weave in and out of the forest hunting prey. Their prey includes opossums, sloths, and monkeys.

Ruby-throated Hummingbirds winter in tropical forests. They have a long, slender bill for collecting nectar. They are often seen hovering near tubular flowers.

Scarlet Macaws live in wild forests in Central and South America. They are stunning birds with bright red, yellow, blue, and green wing and tail feathers. They have a large, curved, powerful beak for breaking through the husks of rainforest fruits. They don't spread seeds like some fruit-eating animals but actually eat or destroy the seeds.

Toucans live in lowland forests from southern Mexico to northern South America. They have a giant, hollow bill with which they pluck fruit. Then they flip their heads back and gulp the fruit down. They spit out the seeds, which helps to spread them.

Amazon Rainforest Butterflies

Glasswing Butterflies fly close to the ground in the forest. Their delicate, transparent wings often are decorated with eyespots.

Julia Butterflies are found in clearings and along the margins of the forest. They are fast fliers feeding on nectar. They also seek out minerals from puddles and water droplets pooling on reptiles.

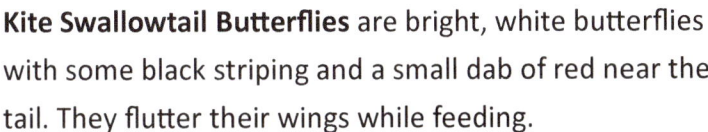

Kite Swallowtail Butterflies are bright, white butterflies with some black striping and a small dab of red near the tail. They flutter their wings while feeding.

Morpho Butterflies are huge and bright iridescent blue. They feed on rotting fruit on the forest floor.

Owl Butterflies are big, brown butterflies with large eye spots on their back wings. They feed on rotting fruit on the forest floor.

Sulfur Butterflies gather around puddles of water to sip on dissolved minerals found on the forest floor and even from water pooling on turtles or other reptiles.

At Eifrig Publishing, our motto is our mission —
"Good for our kids, good for our Earth,
and good for our communities."

We are passionate about helping kids develop into caring, creative, thoughtful individuals who possess positive self-images, celebrate differences, and practice inclusion. Our books promote social and environmental consciousness and empower children as they grow in their communities.

© 2022 Sheri Amsel
Edited by Jason Gruhl and Brianna Peterson
Printed in the United States of America

All rights reserved. This publication is protected by Copyright, and permission should be obtained from the publisher prior to any prohibited reproduction, storage in a retrieval system, or transmission in any form or by any means, electronic, mechanical, photocopying, recording, or likewise.

Published by Eifrig Publishing,
PO Box 66, Lemont, PA 16851, USA
Knobelsdorffstr. 44, 14059 Berlin, Germany.
For information regarding permission, write to:

Rights and Permissions Department,
Eifrig Publishing, PO Box 66, Lemont, PA 16851, USA.
permissions@eifrigpublishing.com, +1-888-340-6543

Library of Congress Cataloging-in-Publication Data

Amsel, Sheri
The Rodent, the Bee, and the Brazil Nut Tree
by Sheri Amsel

p. cm.

Paperback: ISBN 978-1-63233-322-3
Hard cover: ISBN 978-1-63233-323-0
Ebook: ISBN 978-1-63233-324-7

[1. Science-Nature - Juvenile Non-Fiction.

2. Animals - Juvenile Non-Fiction]
I. Amsel, Sheri , ill. II. Title

26 25 24 23 2022

5 4 3 2 1

Printed on recycled acid-free paper. ∞